Waste and Recycling

Sally Hewitt

Crabtree Publishing Company
www.crabtreebooks.com

Crabtree Publishing Company
www.crabtreebooks.com

Author: Sally Hewitt
Editors: Jeremy Smith, Molly Aloian
Proofreaders: Adrianna Morganelli, Crystal Sikkens
Project editor: Robert Walker
Production coordinator: Margaret Amy Salter
Art director: Jonathan Hair
Design: Jason Anscomb
Prepress technician: Katherine Berti

Activity pages development by Shakespeare Squared
www.shakespearesquared.com

Library and Archives Canada Cataloguing in Publication

Hewitt, Sally, 1949-
    Waste and recycling / Sally Hewitt.

(Green team)
Include index.
ISBN 978-0-7787-4098-8 (bound).--ISBN 978-0-7787-4105-3 (pbk.)

    1. Recycling (Waste, etc.)--Juvenile literature. 2. Refuse and refuse disposal--Juvenile literature. I. Title. II. Series: Hewitt, Sally, 1949- .. Green team.

TD792.H49 2008   j363.72'82   C2008-903492-9

Library of Congress Cataloging-in-Publication Data

Hewitt, Sally, 1949-
  Waste and recycling / Sally Hewitt.
    p. cm. -- (Green team)
  Includes index.
  ISBN-13: 978-0-7787-4105-3 (pbk. : alk. paper)
  ISBN-10: 0-7787-4105-2 (pbk. : alk. paper)
  ISBN-13: 978-0-7787-4098-8 (reinforced library binding : alk. paper)
  ISBN-10: 0-7787-4098-6 (reinforced library binding : alk. paper)
  1. Refuse and refuse disposal--Juvenile literature. 2. Recycling (Waste, etc.)--Juvenile literature. I. Title. II. Series.

TD792.H49 2008
363.72'82--dc22
                        2008023290

Crabtree Publishing Company
www.crabtreebooks.com   1-800-387-7650

Printed in the U.S.A./052013/BS20130507

Published in Canada
Crabtree Publishing
616 Welland Ave.
St. Catharines, Ontario
L2M 5V6

Published in the United States
Crabtree Publishing
PMB 59051
350 Fifth Ave., 59th Floor
New York, NY 10118

Contents

Recycling

There is always an important question to ask before throwing something away; can I reduce the waste I make by reusing or **recycling** it? If you cannot reuse it, then you can save energy and materials and keep the waste out of **landfills** by recycling it.

What is recycling?

Recycling means breaking down items such as clothes, computers, cans, or bottles, and using the materials and parts to make something new. Recycling uses energy but uses less energy than making something new from raw materials.

Rubber tires are shredded and turned into grains of rubber, which can be used again and made into rubber goods at this tire recycling plant.

Look out for this logo before you throw something away. It tells you "this can be recycled."

Different types of materials

Everything we use is made of some kind of material. Raw materials are natural materials, such as rubber, metal, and wood, that can be made into things such as tires, cans, or paper. Man-made materials are made from raw materials. For example, plastic is made from oil. Materials can be divided into two groups —nonrenewable and renewable.

Nonrenewable materials

Some raw materials are not renewable. One day, they will run out because we have used them up. Oil is nonrenewable. It is drawn up from deep under the earth or sea and used for fuel and to make plastic. Bauxite is also nonrenewable. It is used to make aluminium for cooking foil and drinking cans (see pages 18-19).

Renewable materials

Some materials can be renewed because they come from living things. If they are carefully managed, they will not run out. Cotton is renewable. It can be harvested and replanted. A sheep's woolly coat will grow again after it has been shorn. Wood comes from trees and new trees can be planted.

Newspapers are **biodegradable**. They are printed on paper, which is made from wood. They are recyclable, too. They can be broken down and made into clean paper again.

Lucy

The plastic bottle Lucy is drinking from can be recycled. Oil will be saved by recycling the bottle and using the plastic again.

Paper and cardboard

All kinds of different things that we use every day are made of paper or cardboard. We often use them just once, then throw them away. Throwing away paper and cardboard should be the last thing we do when we need to get rid of them.

school book

tissue

newspaper

Which of these things do you use the most? What do you do with them when you have finished with them?

Garbage!

Most household, school, and business garbage is paper and cardboard. Paper and cardboard do not have to go in the trash can, however.

Paper is recyclable

Even though paper and cardboard are made from wood, which is a renewable material, it makes sense to recycle paper. If you recycle it, you will save the energy that goes into making paper from wood.

Challenge!

Reduce your garbage by about one-third.

- Do not put any paper or cardboard in the trash can!
- Take out paperclips, staples, string, glue, and paper with a shiny, waterproof coating. What you have left will be "clean" waste paper, which is a good material for making new paper.

The children of Potter Street Elementary School won the American Forest and Paper Association recycling award for their "We Always Recycle" program.

Ian **Lisa** **Pip**

We're recycling old Yellow Pages directories here

www.yellow-woods.com

Children collect Yellow Pages for recycling. They can be turned into animal bedding, cardboard, padded envelopes, egg cartons, and insulation.

Case study—Potter Street Elementary, Georgia

Everyone at Potter Street Elementary School in Georgia takes part in its recycling program. In just six months, they collected 10,000 pounds (4,536 kg) of paper and sent it to be recycled. They have made a difference! The school saves money by not having to pay for as much garbage to be taken away. They have also been awarded a grant to help them with their good work.

The Yellow Woods Challenge

Yellow Pages and The Woodland Trust runs the Yellow Woods Challenge. Yellow Pages make telephone books. In the United Kingdom, they give cash prizes to schools for recycling old books. For every pound of prize money, they give a pound to The Woodland Trust.

The trust puts it toward their "Tree For All" campaign. The aim is to plant twelve million trees over a five-year period—that is one for every child under sixteen in the UK.

Action!

Save and recycle paper at school.

- Use both sides of the paper.
- Do not put paper in the recycling bin if you can still use it!
- Put a paper collection box in every classroom.
- Find an organization such as the American Forest and Paper Association who will work with you.
- Make sure your school buys recycled paper goods.
- Take a cotton handkerchief to school rather than using tissues.

Organic waste

Garden waste and food scraps are **organic waste**, which means waste from living things. Organic waste naturally breaks down and can be put back into the soil as **compost**.

Organic waste can be recycled. It will turn into compost.

Challenge!

At home and at school, make sure all your organic waste is collected for recycling or turned into compost.

• Find out if food waste and garden waste can be collected for recycling in your area.

• If not, turn it into compost or ask someone with a garden to turn it into compost for you.

What is organic waste?

Organic waste is all the food waste we throw away. Although all food waste will break down, it is best to avoid adding cooked meat to compost as this attracts animals. Food waste makes up a large amount of our garbage. Uncooked fruit and vegetable scraps, tea bags, and coffee granules, mixed with garden weeds, grass cuttings, pet litter, and some paper, make good compost for the garden.

If we do not recycle the organic waste, it all goes to a landfill, where it biodegrades and makes a liquid that seeps into the soil and water. This can cause **pollution**.

Animal waste

People and animals make organic waste, too. Human waste is called sewage. Animal waste is called manure. It is a natural compost often added to soil to make it more fertile.

Charlize

Charlynn

Chanel

Students at Rocklands Primary School look at compost produced by their earthworm factory.

Case study—A wormery in South Africa

At Rocklands Primary, a small school in Mitchells Plain, South Africa, students and staff are developing a vegetable garden. Students and staff bring vegetable peels from home and add them to the school's composting "bath" and earthworm factories. The worms produce a rich compost that is perfect for helping garden plants grow quickly.

Case study—Elephant dung

The Maximus Elephant Conservation Trust and Foundation turns elephant dung (manure) into paper (see right). First, the dung is boiled and steamed to kill germs. The dung is then turned into pulp, which is made into paper.

Action!

Make a **wormery**.

- You need a big wooden or plastic box with a lid and about 100 worms. You can buy them from fishing tackle shops or collect them yourself.
- To make the bedding, line the bottom of the box with torn up newspaper, compost, and leaf mold. Sprinkle it with water.
- Add organic waste and crushed egg shells.
- Cover with bedding and put in the worms.
- Keep the lid on and your compost will be ready in about three months.
- When you want to harvest your compost, shine a torch onto the wormery. This makes the worms wriggle down to the bottom.
- Take out the compost and use it in pots, tubs, and gardens to make your school environment a better, more beautiful place that is rich in wildlife.

Paper pulp made from elephant dung is spread out to dry. After this, it will be ready to use!

Cooking oil

The cooking oil we use for frying, stir-frying, and making salad dressing all comes from plants. It is made by pressing seeds and nuts to take out their oils.

People grow corn as a food and produce vegetable oil from its seeds.

Biofuel

Oil for cooking comes from many different types of crops. This oil can also be made into a kind of fuel called biofuel. Biofuel means fuel made from plants. It is renewable because it comes from crops that can be grown again. Biofuel will not run out.

Greenhouse gas

Burning biofuels releases a dangerous **greenhouse gas** called carbon dioxide. The gas is released into the air. The plants that biofuels are made from take in carbon dioxide as they grow. This helps to balance the amount of carbon dioxide in the air.

A growing desire for biofuel means that more and more forests are being cleared to grow biofuel crops.

This is the logo of the Slick Schools program in Brighton, which collects used cooking oil from schools and turns it into biofuel.

Biofuel problems

Crops for biofuel can cause problems. If farmers grow biofuel crops instead of food, people may go hungry. Forests are cleared to grow biofuels. Making biofuels uses more energy than the energy they actually supply.

Do not throw it away!

When you pour away used cooking oil, it can block up drains and contaminate the water system. You do not have to throw it away. It can be recycled and turned into biofuel.

Case study— Recycling cooking oil

Seven eco-schools in Brighton, Sussex, in England, have joined a program called Slick Schools. They collect cooking oil for recycling into biofuel. Used cooking oil from the school kitchen and from students' homes is collected and stored in a lockable oil bin. Twice a term, the bins are opened for other people and restaurants to bring along their used cooking oil.

Action!

Collect cooking oil at home and at school for recycling.

- Oil must be vegetable oil for cooking, not any other kind of oil.
- Vegetable oil mixed with animal fat or water is not suitable.
- Bits of food do not matter. They will be sieved out.

Challenge!

Find out if there is a program or company like Slick Schools near you that will collect used cooking oil and recycle it into biofuel. If so, find out if your school is willing to get involved.

Textiles

Clothes, shoes, blankets, and duvets are all made of different kinds of **textiles**. When you have finished with them, they can be cleaned, mended, and reused if they are in good enough condition. If not, textiles can be recycled. They do not have to be thrown away.

What do you do with your clothes when you have grown out of them or when they get torn or stained? Many people shop for clothes in secondhand stores because the clothes are still in good condition and are sold at a low price.

What happens to textiles sent for recycling?

If you send your textiles to a charity, first they will be sorted. Things in good condition are sent all over the world to people who can make good use of them. Textiles that cannot be reused are recycled. Wool clothes are made into yarn to make fabric. Silk and cotton are made into wiping cloths. Other clothes are shredded and made into materials used for padding and lining things such as roofs and furniture.

Challenge!

Do not leave unused clothes, shoes, belts, bags, and bedding lying around the house.

Sort them into piles:

- things you can use again
- things that someone else can use
- things that can be cleaned, mended, and used again
- things to be recycled

Now make sure everything is reused or recycled!

Meadowbrook Elementary School in Chicago collected the most textiles and won the cash prize for their school.

Design clothes that are good for the planet.

- Have fun and use your imagination!
- Think about what the clothes will be made of.
- Will the material last forever or will it be biodegradable?
- Maybe you can eat your clothes when you have finished with them!
- Can the clothes become something else?
- What can the material be recycled into?

Case study— recycling competition

Schools in the Chicago area joined in a contest to collect the most textiles for recycling. The company U'SAgain provided recycling boxes for the school grounds. Anyone from the area could drop off clothes and shoes for recycling. Each school that took part received $40 for every ton of textiles they collected.

Imagination

Old clothes can be recycled in all kinds of imaginative ways. One company recycles old denim jeans and turns them into shoes and sandals, so you can wear your old jeans on your feet! Unsold jeans from secondhand stores and warehouses are bought and turned into shoes and sandals. Using denim that has already been manufactured helps to save energy and look after the planet.

You can recycle natural fibers such as wool, cotton, and silk by cutting them into pieces and adding them in small amounts to the compost heap.

Old denim can be turned into a new pair of shoes, like this pair above.

Plastic

The raw material used to make plastic is oil, a **fossil fuel** that will run out one day. Some plastic is biodegradable—it will break down and become part of the soil or ground again—but most plastic will stay around and pollute the soil, water, and air.

Plastic can be recycled but it needs to be sorted first because each kind of plastic is recycled separately.

Some plastic rings for drinking cans are photodegradable.

Look out for a number inside a recycling triangle stamped on plastic items.

It tells you what kind of plastic it is made of and if it can be recycled.

1—Drinking bottles
2—Milk and dishsoap liquid containers
3—Food trays and shampoo bottles
4—Plastic bags

Photodegradable plastic

There is a kind of plastic called **photodegradable** plastic. This plastic is better for the environment because it breaks down in sunlight. Photodegradable plastic can also be recycled.

Challenge!

Do not throw plastic away!

- Sort and recycle plastic by numbers.
- Numbers 1 and 2 can be recycled more easily (see page 16).
- Remove the plastic top then wash and squash.
- Supermarkets often have a recycling bin for plastic bags.
- Reduce your use of plastic items that can not be recycled.

Plastic and landfill sites

If we throw plastic away, it eventually ends up in a landfill. Photodegrable plastic will eventually break down. A new generation of plastic bags with corn starch or vegetable oil added to them will also biodegrade. Many plastic bags will never break down, and we should try and reuse these.

Action!

Have a plastic bag collection at school.

- Get everyone to bring their plastic bags from home.
- Deal them out.
- How many times and how many different ways can you reuse each bag?
- Use your imagination and share your ideas.
- When the bags are worn out, take them back to the store for recycling.
- Take cloth bags shopping when all the plastic bags are used up.

This steamroller is making a new road surface from ash produced by burning plastic.

Waste to energy

Plastic is made from oil, a fossil fuel. If plastic is burned, it can be turned back into energy to make electricity! The smoke has to be cleaned before it can be released into the air. Once the ash has been checked for pollutants, it can be used to build roads and to make other building materials.

Metal

Metal is a raw material mined from rocks and earth. It is nonrenewable. Valuable metals are hardly ever thrown away, but people all over the world throw away millions of food and drinking cans made of steel and aluminium every day.

Millions of soda cans are produced every year. They take a lot of energy to make, so do not throw them away.

Challenge!

Recycle cans!

- If you buy a can of soda when you are out and there is nowhere to recycle it, take it home and put it in your recycling bin.
- Squash aluminium soda cans so they take up less space.
- Rinse steel food cans such as cans of baked beans and soup.

Aluminium and steel

Soda cans are made from aluminium and food cans are made from steel. If they are thrown away, they become scrap metal. Aluminium and steel scrap metal is valuable and can be recycled. It does not make sense to throw it away. Steel can be picked out of garbage by giant magnets and recycled, but aluminium is not magnetic. It needs to be put in the recycling bin.

In Cyprus, one recycling program has collected more than 16 million cans. Their value has paid for all the equipment for the Makarios Hospital in Nicosia.

Case study—Cans For Kids

Cans For Kids is a registered charity, formed in 1990 to organize the collection and recycling of aluminium cans in Cyprus. The charity uses the proceeds from recycling to purchase medical equipment for the children's wards at Cypriot hospitals. Cans For Kids raises awareness of the benefits of recycling by visiting schools to give talks and show the Cans For Kids video explaining why we should recycle aluminium.

Aluminuium oxide is being smelted into metal bars.

Making a new aluminium can

It takes a lot to create a new can. A raw material called "bauxite" is mined, then taken to a mill and turned into aluminium oxide. This is then shipped across the water for thousands of kilometres to a hydroelectric plant. Here, it is melted down into metal bars. The bars are then shipped to another country where they are rolled into sheets before arriving in the country they will be used in. Once the sheets get there, they are formed into cans, sent to a bottler to be filled with soda, and then delivered to stores.

In the UK, most of the bauxite in a can comes all the way from Australia and shipped to hydroelectric plants in Scandinavia. In the United States, bauxite is mined in Jamaica and South America, and processed in North America.

Recycling a can

Cans can usually be recycled without taking such a long journey. Cans are taken from the recycling center to a scrap processing company where they are crushed into briquettes. These are then delivered to the aluminium company where they are stripped of paint, shredded, melted, and blended with new aluminium and rolled into sheets. These sheets are then delivered to a can maker, sent off to be filled with soda and then delivered to stores! This uses far less energy—both in making the aluminium and transporting it.

Action!

Hold a school assembly.

Use these facts to convince students and staff to recycle cans:

- One recycled can saves enough energy to run a television for three hours.
- If all cans were recycled, it would save huge amounts of landfill space.
- What other facts can you find to support your argument?

Glass

Even though glass is made of natural raw materials including sand, soda ash, and limestone, it is not biodegradable. Once glass has been made, it never breaks down.

These glass items were made thousands of years ago. They can tell us about how people lived in the past.

Recyclable glass

Drinks and sauces come in glass bottles. Jam and honey come in glass jars. When they are empty, we often throw them away. But glass can be recycled over and over again and still make good quality glass. First, the glass is crushed into small pieces. Then it is sent to a glass factory where it is mixed with sand, soda ash, and limestone, and made into new bottles and jars. Fewer raw materials and less energy are needed to make recycled glass than new glass.

Non-recyclable glass

Not all glass can be recycled. Glass light bulbs, glass cooking pots, mirrors, and window panes are not recyclable because other material has been added to the glass they are made of.

Action!

Never throw away recyclable glass again!

Glass buried underground in landfills is there forever.

- Recycle glass at home and at school.
- Put it out for roadside collection.
- Take it to a recycling center.

Case study— Glass Forever

Glass Forever is a roadshow that visits schools and teaches students about recycling glass. The children learn why recycling glass is good for the planet, how it is recycled, and what they can do to get involved. The roadshow visited Chetwood Primary School in the UK, and was a great success.

The children got to see glass being recycled into new bottles at a glass factory.

Paula

Andy

Andy and Paula learned to recycle glass at their local recycling center.

Viv Hodges, Head Teacher of Chetwood Primary, says: "The children particularly enjoyed the sorting machine. The children are currently doing followup work on the theme of glass recycling."

Children at Chetwood Primary learned how a glass recycling machine works.

Challenge!

Recycle glass and save the planet!

- The energy saved recycling one glass bottle could light a 100 watt light bulb for four hours!
- Only half the amount of greenhouse gases are made when glass is made from recycled glass than when glass is produced from raw materials.
- Fewer raw materials are used up when glass is recycled.

Cellular phones

Today, we cannot imagine life without cellular phones. When a new design comes on the market, many people buy it and get rid of the old one that probably still works perfectly well.

Modern technology lets us chat to friends, listen to music, check the latest news, and play computer games, wherever we are.

Old cellular phones

What happens to our old cellular phones? They often get pushed to the back of a drawer or left in the bottom of a cupboard. If your old cellular phone is in a drawer, do not leave it there. It is valuable. It can either be used again, mended if it is broken, or recycled.

Throwing away cellulars

Cellular phones contain dangerous **chemicals** that are harmful to the environment. When a cellular phone is thrown away, it goes to a landfill site where it starts to break down. The poisonous chemicals leak into the soil and then into water. The plastic case and metals it is made of are wasted. They could be recycled and used again.

Challenge!

Look all around your house for unused cellular phones.

• Ask an adult how to get rid of them in a way that is good for the planet.

Valuable materials are **recovered** and recycled at this cellular phone recycling factory.

Recycling cellular phones

When cellular phones are recycled, the harmful chemicals are disposed of safely. Tiny amounts of precious metals, gold, silver, and platinum are saved and used for jewelry. Copper and nickel are used to make stainless steel products such as saucepans and knives. Plastic is ground down and made into traffic cones.

Being responsible

Unused cellular phones can be sent back to the manufacturer for recycling. You can also collect old cellular phones, win a prize for your school, and help to save the planet at the same time! Organizations will collect cellular phones from schools and youth organizations. Prizes are given in return.

Fones4schools is an organization in the UK that helps stop old cellular phones from going into landfills.

Big machines

Millions of people all over the world cannot imagine life without a car. They depend on their cars to get to work, to go to school, and to go to stores.

This old car has been dumped, burned, and left in the middle of the countryside.

Cars pump gases into the atmosphere that cause air pollution and global warming.

What happens to old cars?

When cars are about 14 years old, they usually reach the end of their lives and they are either scrapped or dumped.

Scrapped!

When cars are scrapped, three-quarters of their weight is reused and recycled.
- Aluminium and steel are recovered and recycled.
- Rubber tires are shredded and recycled.
- The working parts are resold and used again.
- Fuel, oil, and antifreeze are all recovered and recycled.

If your family car is ready for the junkyard:

- Make sure it is taken to a junkyard where as much as possible is recycled.
- Find out where the parts can be recycled and disposed of safely.

Dumped!

When cars are dumped, everything goes to waste and the environment is damaged.
- All the valuable materials they are made from are wasted.
- The working parts become useless.
- Fuel, oil, and antifreeze cause pollution.

White goods

Fridges, freezers, stoves, washing machines, dryers, and dishwashers are called white goods because they are usually white. They are big machines that can cause pollution if they are not disposed of and recycled properly.

Action!

If your family or school needs to get rid of a fridge or another big machine, be sure to dispose of it responsibly.

- Make sure it is clean and empty.
- If it is reusable, find who will collect it for reuse.
- If it is going to be recycled, check that harmful substances will be disposed of safely and that metal and plastic will be shredded and recycled.

CFCs and the ozone layer

Old fridges and freezers contain CFCs— harmful substances that can damage the **ozone layer**. The ozone layer in Earth's atmosphere protects us from the sun's harmful rays. If it is badly damaged, life on Earth is threatened. Now CFCs are banned but other less harmful gases still should be disposed of safely.

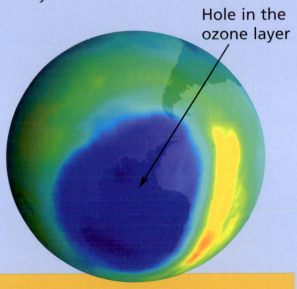

Hole in the ozone layer

This photo taken from space shows the hole in the ozone layer. Scientists hope the ozone layer will repair itself in 50 to 60 years.

Old appliances in working condition can be used again by someone else. Others need to be correctly recycled.

A recycling party

A recycling party is a great way of putting all you have learned about recycling into practice. You can have fun with your friends and make sure you do not harm the planet at the same time.

Dress up in clothes made out of recyclable materials with a recycling theme, such as this party held at a school.

Recycling in costumes

You could ask your guests to come dressed up in costumes with a recycling theme that encourages everyone to recycle! The costumes should all be made from things around the house. Do not buy anything new to make them.

This costume and sign were made from things found around the house.

Challenge!

Throw a party and make very little or no waste!

• Buy or make recycled paper invitations and party bags.
• Make the party food at home.
• Bake your own cake, make your own sandwiches, serve raw vegetable sticks, and fresh fruit chunks.
• Fill the party bags with homemade gifts or gifts made from recycled material.
• Compost or recycle any waste.

Bags of garbage

At the end of a party, big black bags are often filled with garbage and thrown away. Everything made of paper and cardboard can be rinsed and recycled several times. Foil can be washed and used again or recycled. If you use china or plastic plates and mugs, metal forks and spoons, and cloth tablecloths and napkins, they can all be washed and used again.

This recycled robot costume was made from cardboard boxes, cardboard rolls, and used wrapping paper. It could all be put in the recycling bin after the party!

After this party, all the paper and cardboard was sent off for recycling.

Action!

Make a recycled robot costume from old boxes.

• Do not buy anything new!
• You need a small cardboard box, a large cardboard box, old wrapping paper, and glue.
• Cut out a square for your face in the small box.
• Cut holes for your arms in the sides of the big box and a hole for your head in the top.
• Stick the boxes together and cover them with wrapping paper.
• Use your imagination. You could decorate your robot with things that can be recycled.

Join the recycling revolution

Help set up and take care of recycling bins at your house.

Let's Get Started!

We know that recycling is good for the planet. Recycling keeps material out of landfills. It also saves energy. But many people do not recycle. Some families have no time to set up recycling bins. Some areas do not have curbside pickup. Whatever the case, you can help your household recycle. If you already recycle, show a neighbor or relative how it's done!

Activity

1. Hold a family meeting. Tell your parent or guardian that you want to start recycling at home. Explain why recycling is good for the Earth.

2. If he or she agrees, find out if there is curbside pickup in your area. Some towns hire a company to pick up recyclables from houses. Ask an adult at home to consider calling and signing up for this service.

3. Another idea is to use city collection sites. Call your city's information number and ask where the sites are located. Many areas put recycling containers in parks and parking lots. People put their recyclables in these containers. The city takes the material to a recycling center.

4. Sometimes the pickup company gives customers recycling bins. But you can make your own bins, too. You can use large plastic boxes with lids. Another idea is to line large, sturdy cardboard boxes with plastic. Use these boxes for empty food or drink containers, such as soda cans, or old pizza boxes. You can use cardboard boxes or paper bags to recycle newspapers and magazines.

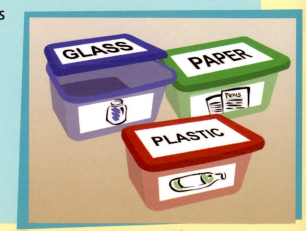

5. Make a label for each bin. The label should tell what belongs in the bin. If you live with young children, you can add pictures to the labels.

6. Find a good place to put your recycling bins. Many families put bins outside or in the garage.

7. After every meal, put recyclables in the bins. Rinse out food containers to keep animals away from the bins. Watch for other recyclables around the house. Empty shampoo bottles and toilet paper tubes can be recycled.

8. Take the bins to the curb on pickup day. Or help your family take them to a city collection site.

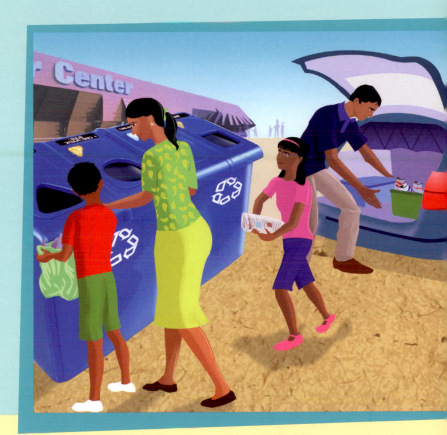

Looking Back

After your family has been recycling for a while, talk about how your system is working.

• How much does recycling reduce the trash your family throws away?

• What can you do to make recycling easier?

• How can you recycle even more?

Your family might decide to encourage others in your community to recycle, too. You could tell your neighbors about recycling. Or you could ask your city to provide curbside pickup if your area does not have it.

Glossary

Biodegradable
When something is biodegradable, it breaks down naturally and becomes part of the soil, water, or air. Vegetable peels are biodegradable. Most plastic is not.

Chemicals
Chemicals are substances we use for all kinds of things, including cleaning, cooking, and killing pests. Some chemicals can damage the environment.

Compost
Compost is decayed organic material such as plants, food waste, and paper. It can be dug into the soil to make it richer and better for growing things.

Fossil fuel
A fuel that is made from the ancient remains of an animal or plant.

Greenhouse gas
A gas such as carbon dioxide that leads to the warming of Earth's surface.

Landfill
A way of getting rid of waste by burying it in the ground.

Ozone layer
A layer high up in the atmosphere that protects Earth from the harmful rays of the sun.

Organic waste
Food waste that naturally breaks down and can be put back into the soil as compost.

Photodegradable
Photodegradable material can be broken down into sunlight.

Pollution
A substance in the environment that is harmful or poisonous. Exhaust fumes from cars pollute the air. Oil spills at sea pollute the water.

Recover
When useful materials or working parts are saved and taken out of things that have been thrown away, we say they have been recovered.

Recycling
Recycling something means to break it down and use the material and working parts to make something new.

Textile
A textile is a cloth or fabric made by weaving or knitting yarn or thread.

Wormery
A wormery uses worms to help break down organic material such as food and plants to make compost.

Websites

www.woodland-trust.org.uk/yell
The Woodland Trust is the UK's leading woodland conservation charity. It is working with Yell, the publisher of Yellow Pages directories, on the Yellow Woods Challenge, helping children to recycle Yellow Pages directories and win cash prizes for their schools.

www.magpie.coop/slick_schools.php
Slick Schools is an organization that collect waste oil from schools and transforms it into environmentally-friendly biofuel.

www.fones4schools.co.uk
Fones4Schools is the leading UK recycling campaign for schools and groups of any kind. Fones4Schools works with thousands of schools across the UK and helps to raise money for participants.

www.olliesworld.com
A website for children to learn to reduce, reuse, and recycle.

www.eco-schools.org
Your school can become part of a group of schools committed to saving the planet and caring for the environment.

Note to parents and teachers:
Every effort has been made by the Publishers to ensure that these websites are suitable for children, that they are of the highest educational value, and that they contain no inappropriate or offensive material. However, because of the nature of the Internet, it is impossible to guarantee that the contents of these sites will not be altered. We strongly advise that Internet access is supervised by a responsible adult.

Index